PRESENTS

Wiggles
First Day of School

This is Wiggles.

AaBbCcDdEeFf

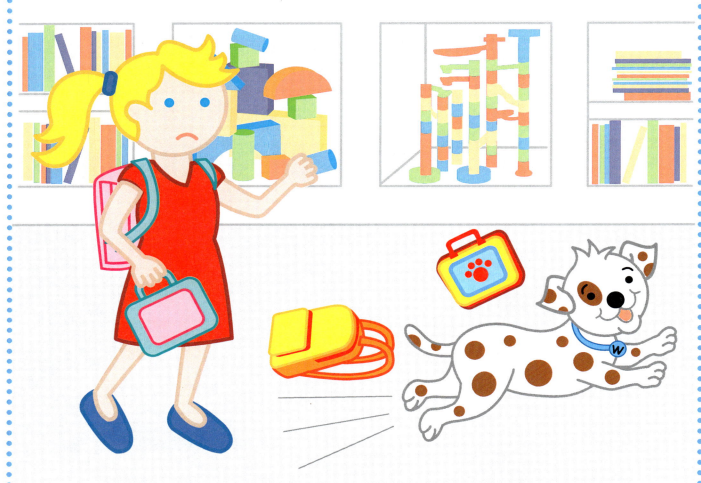

Wiggles was so excited! He dropped his backpack and lunchbox on the floor and ran off to play.

And the children said,
"No, no, Wiggles!
Put your things away!"

The teacher said, "Everyone raise your right hand." Wiggles tried, but it was his left paw, not his right!

And the children said,
"No, no, Wiggles!
Raise your right paw!"

Then the teacher showed everyone a calendar.
She said, "What month is it?"
And Wiggles said, "Tuesday!"

And the children said,
"No, no, Wiggles!
Tuesday is a day, not a month!"

Wiggles said, "It's too hard!
I can't remember!"

And the children said,
"No, no, Wiggles!
Just try your best!"

The teacher started to read a story. Wiggles raised his paw. She called on him and he said, "I have this book at home!"

And the children said,
"No, no, Wiggles!
That's a story, not a question!"

Then the teacher said that it was time to go outside to play. Wiggles started barking and jumping up and down!

And the children said,
"No, no, Wiggles!
Use a quiet voice inside!"

On the way out the door, the teacher gave the children a snack. Wiggles took it and ran out the door.

And the children said,
"No, no, Wiggles! Start with 'please' and then say 'thank you!'"

When it was time to come inside, the bell rang. All of the children froze when they heard the bell ring, but not Wiggles!

And the children said, "No, no, Wiggles! When the bell rings, freeze! Stop! Hands up!"

The children sat down for a story, but Wiggles kept squirming! The teacher said, "Wiggles, do you need to go to the restroom?" And he said, "No, I don't want to!"

And the children said, "No, no, Wiggles! When you're doing the potty dance, it's time to go!" And the teacher said, "Potty, potty, flush, flush. Wash, wash, hush, hush!"

When Wiggles came back, the class had started an art project, so Wiggles got out the glue. He liked glue, so he put on lots and LOTS!

And the children said,
"No, no, Wiggles!
Just a dot, not a lot! One dot!"

When he was all done with his art project, Wiggles put his things away, but forgot to put the cap on his marker.

And the children said,
"No, no, Wiggles!
Snap that cap!"

Then Wiggles saw a little girl walk away from her marker, forgetting to put the cap on. And Wiggles said, "TEACHER!!!!! She didn't put the cap on her marker!!!"

And the children said, "No, no, Wiggles! Nobody likes a tattletale!" And the teacher said, "That's not an emergency, Wiggles! Next time, just remind her to put the cap on."

When it was time for lunch, the teacher told the children to line up at the door. Wiggles and a few other children raced for the door, and started fighting for the front of the line!

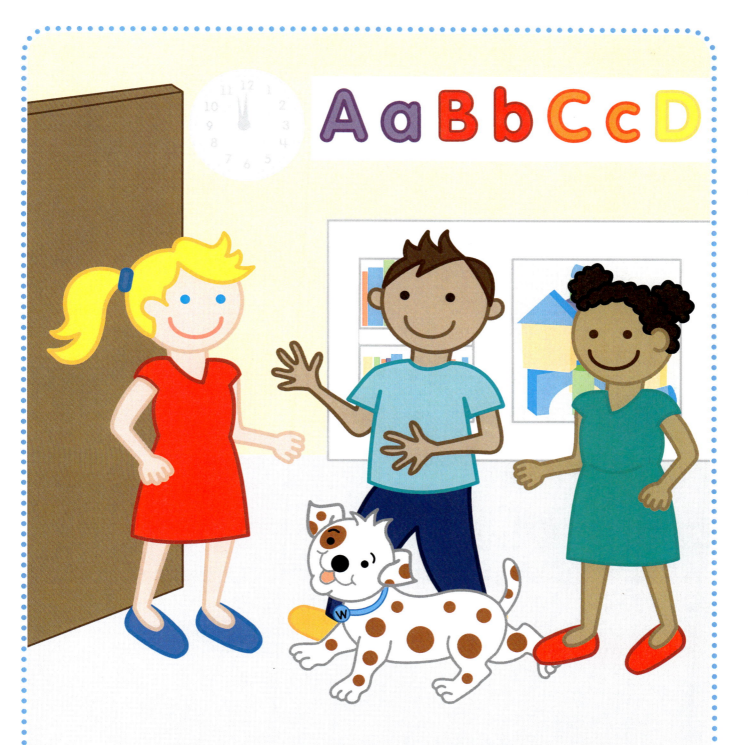

And the other children said,
"No, no, Wiggles!
We don't fight!"

When everyone was in line, the teacher led them to the cafeteria. The teacher taught them a song as they walked along, just for fun!

Wiggles was happy because he had his brand new lunchbox, lots of friends, and he loved his nice, new teacher! Wiggles liked school!

The End.

Wiggles went to school. It was his very first day!

Wiggles
First Day of School

Name: _____

And the children said, "No, no, Wiggles! Put your things away!"

Wiggles was so excited! He dropped his backpack and lunchbox on the floor and ran off to play.

And the children said, "No, no, Wiggles! Raise your right paw!"

The teacher said, "Everyone raise your right hand." Wiggles tried, but it was his left paw, not his right!

And the children said, "No, no, Wiggles! Tuesday is a day, not a month!"

Then the teacher showed everyone a calendar. She said, "What month is it?" And Wiggles said, "Tuesday!"

And the children said,
"No, no, Wiggles!
Just try your best!"

Wiggles said,
"It's too hard!
I can't remember!"

And the children said, "No, no, Wiggles! That's a story, not a question!"

The teacher started to read a story. Wiggles raised his paw. She called on him and he said, "I have this book at home!"

And the children said,
"No, no, Wiggles!
Use a quiet voice inside!"

Then the teacher said
that it was time to go
outside to play. Wiggles
started barking and
jumping up and down!

And the children said, "No, no, Wiggles! Start with 'please' and then say 'thank you!'"

On the way out the door, the teacher gave the children a snack. Wiggles took it and ran out the door.

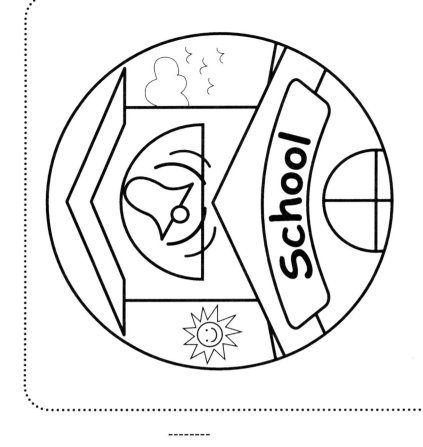

And the children said, "No, no, Wiggles! When the bell rings, freeze! Stop! Hands up!"

When it was time to come inside, the bell rang. All of the children froze when they heard the bell ring, but not Wiggles!

And the children said, "No, no, Wiggles! When you're doing the potty dance, it's time to go!" And the teacher said, "Potty, potty, flush, flush. Wash, wash, hush, hush, hush!"

The children sat down for a story, but Wiggles kept squirming! The teacher said, "Wiggles, do you need to go to the restroom?" He said, "No, I don't want to!"

And the children said, "No, no, Wiggles! Just a dot, not a lot!"

When Wiggles came back, the class had started an art project, so Wiggles got out the glue. He liked glue, so he put on lots and LOTS!

And the children said,
"No, no, Wiggles!
Snap that cap!"

When he was all done
with his art project,
Wiggles put his things
away, but forgot to put
the cap on his marker.

And the children said, "No, no, Wiggles! Nobody likes a tattle-tale!" And the teacher said, "That's not an emergency, Wiggles! Next time, just remind her to put the cap on."

Then Wiggles saw a little girl walk away from her marker, forgetting to put the cap on. And Wiggles said, "TEACHER!!!!! She didn't put the cap on her marker!!!"

And the other children said, "No, no, Wiggles! We don't fight!"

When it was time for lunch, the teacher told the children to line up. Wiggles and a few other children raced for the door, and started fighting for the front of the line!

Wiggles was happy because he had his brand new lunchbox, lots of new friends, and he loved his nice, new teacher! Wiggles liked school!

When everyone was in line, the teacher led them to the cafeteria. The teacher taught them a song as they walked along, just for fun!

www.HeidiSongs.com
P.O. Box 603, La Verne, CA 91750
(909) 331-2090
©2012 Heidi Butkus • info@heidisongs.com

Illustrations by Laurel Lane ©2012 Heidisongs
laurel@laurellanedesign.com

The End.

Wiggles Cut and Glue Project Instructions

There are two different ways to prepare this project. The first way is to cut the paper into squares and rectangles at the sizes indicated below and have the children round off the corners of the papers to form circles out of squares, and ovals out of rectangles, etc. The second way is to copy the patterns provided and let the children cut out the whole pieces (rather than just the corners). I usually use the first of these two methods because there is less cutting for the children, but this generally means more prep work on the part of the teacher.

In either of the two methods, however, you will have to make a tracer for the body of the dog, because it is too long to fit on one 8.5 x 11 piece of paper. I like to find a used file folder and put the dotted line indicated on the fold of the file folder. Trace the body onto the file folder, and then cut out a pattern. Obviously, you will need a tail on only ONE end, so you can cut off the extra tail! Of course, if you think your students will find it easier to make a body by cutting the corners off of a simple rectangle and then adding a separate piece for a tail, then do feel free to change the project as you see fit. Then you will need to decide if you want to pre-trace the body for your students, or if you think they can trace it themselves. If they are going to trace it themselves, then you will need several tracers made for them ahead of time.

Assuming you are using the method in which you provide the pieces for the children already cut to size, then these are the dimensions that you will need:

Body Part	Color	Dimensions	Number Needed
head	white	6" x 6"	1
ears	white	3" x 3"	1, (cut diagonally to make 2)
eyes	black	1" x 1"	2
nose	black	1.5" x 1.5"	1
body, (including the attached tail)	white	8" x 15" (Smaller if tail is separate)	1
tail (if not attached)	white	6" x 1.5"	1
tufts of fur (for top of head)	white	2" x 1" (Or just use the scraps)	1, (cut diagonally to make 2)

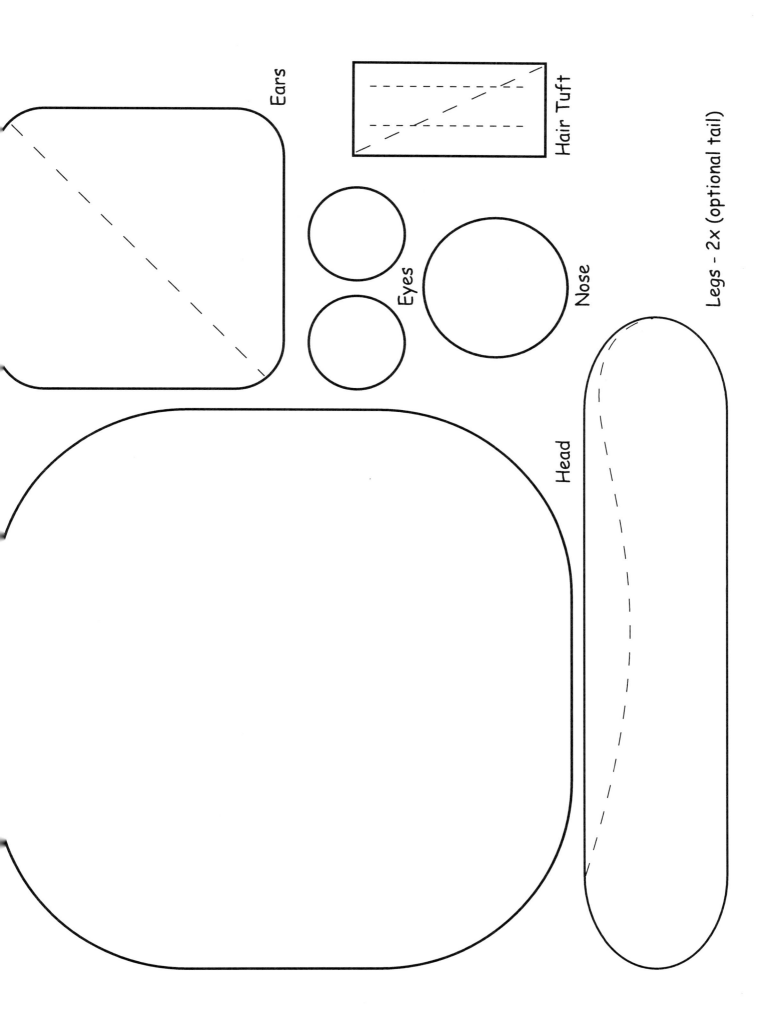

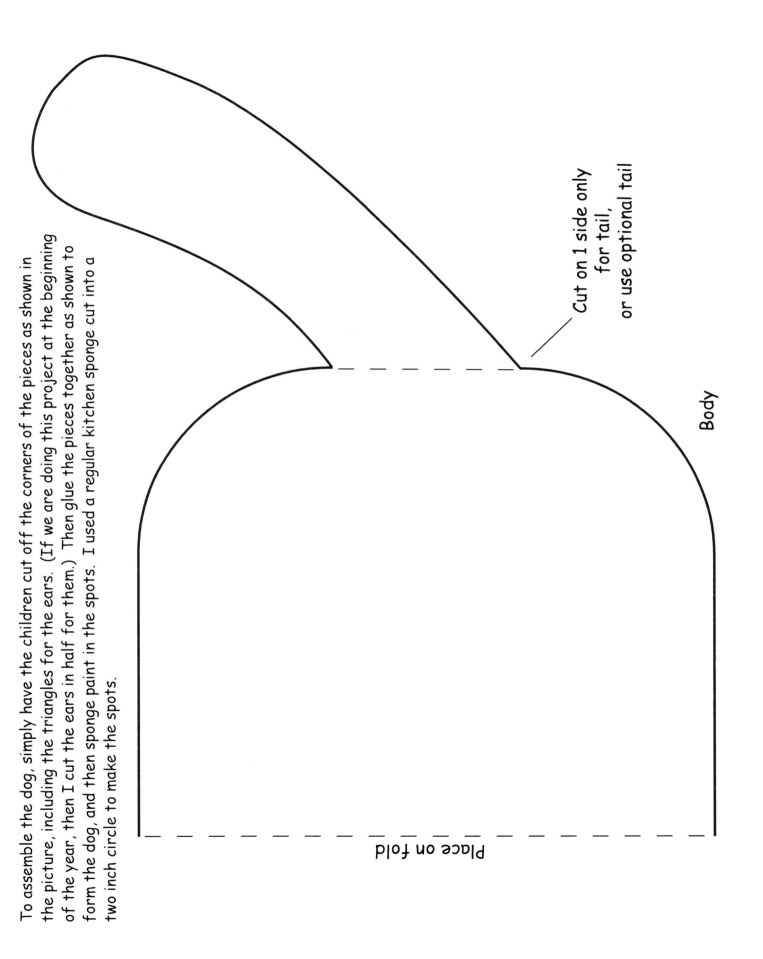

www.HeidiSongs.com
P.O. Box 603, La Verne, CA 91750
(909) 331-2090

©2012 Heidi Butkus • info@heidisongs.com

Illustrations by Laurel Lane ©2012 Heidisongs
laurel@laurellanedesign.com